THE YULETIDE SONG AND

CAROL BOOK

The Yuletide Song and Carol Book

For Religious Liberals who enjoy
singing 4-part (SATB) Harmony,
Songs and Carols for:

ADVENT
CHRISTMAS
YULE & SOLSTICE
ST. STEPHEN'S DAY
WASSAILING & TWELFTH NIGHT
EPIPHANY

✧

Compiled and Edited by:
Dan Harper

fish island press: san mateo, calif. 2014

Copyright © 2014 Dan Harper

Harper, Dan
    The Yuletide song and carol book
    100 pp.   28 cm.
    Includes bibliography and indices.
    ISBN: 978-0-9889413-3-5

FISH ISLAND PRESS
books.fishisland.net

Copyright notice:
    While the texts, melodies, and some of the arrangements in this collection are in the public domain, I retain all rights granted under copyright law, including copyright of the typesetting, editing, any arrangements written by me, and anything else that may be protected under copyright law. This prevents other parties from slapping their own copyright notice on my hard work, and then preventing me from distributing my own work (and yes, Virginia, it has happened to others).
    I hereby grant permission to non-profit organizations such as religious congregations, and to individuals, to make physical printed copies (i.e., photocopies) any of the arrangements in this book, for purposes including congregational singing, small group singing, choir performances, and classes.
    Also, I hereby grant permission to individuals and groups to perform and make audio and video recordings of the arrangements in this book, whether for profit or not for profit, provided that copyright is acknowledged in the audio or video recording.
    N.B.: The musical arrangements are typeset so they may be reduced using a photocopier to fit onto a half sheet, such as might be used as an insert in a congregation's order of service.

Acknowledgements:
    The illustrations are from a nineteenth century Christmas carol book, *Christmas Carols New and Old*, compiled and arr. by Henry R. Bramley and John Stainer (London: Novello, Ewer & Co., 1867), and are in the public domain.

Introduction

This is a collection of Yuletide songs and carols arranged for four voices (SATB). This collection began when a congregation I was serving objected to the degenderized words for "Joy to the World" provided in my denomination's most recent hymnal. The congregation was filled with staunch feminists, but somehow singing "Joy to the world, the Word is come" sounded wrong. This congregation also had a number of people who liked to sing Christmas carols in four-part harmony. Because of this, I began collecting Christmas carols and other seasonal songs, arranged for four voices (soprano, alto, tenor, bass).

That collection led to this book. When deciding whether to put a song in this book, I used the following criteria:

(a) Is this a traditional (or traditional-sounding) song that people would want to sing in December?

(b) Is this a song that religious liberals can sing without gagging on the theology?

(c) Is this a song that's fun and enjoyable to sing in four-part harmony—and not too difficult for the average singer?

A Note on the Music and Texts

I collected most of the songs in this book from older Unitarian, Universalist, American Ethical Union, Quaker, and non-denominational hymnals and songbooks. Note that most Christmas carols and songs have many variants of both text, tune, and arrangements.

For the music, I consulted the hymnals and songbooks in the Bibliography. Where there were variants, I sang through the parts and chose the arrangement that I found most fun to sing. I also consulted some online music resources, such as the hymnsandcarolsofchristmas.com, which contains many page scans of nineteenth century Christmas song books. In one or two cases, I included more than one arrangement of a melody. Some arrangements are adapted from public domain piano or other arrangements.

I have provided *guitar chords* for some of the songs and carols. The guitar chords may not always work perfectly with the SATB arrangement.

For the texts, I relied on older Unitarian, Universalist, American Ethical Union, Quaker, and non-denominational hymnals and songbooks; I also relied on my own judgment. The compilers of hymnals frequently rewrite and alter the texts to hymns and carols, and I looked through many textual variants, occasionally altered a word or two, or dropped a verse that seemed particularly boring or gory (nineteenth century Christmas carols often contain graphic depictions of Jesus' execution). Where space allowed, I have sometimes included as many as thirteen verses.

Note that this collection is not meant to be a scholarly edition of text and tune: it's simply meant to be a collection of both well-known and lesser-known songs that are fun to sing in four-part harmony.

What you'll find in this book is a collection of some four dozen Christmas and seasonal songs. I hope you enjoy singing them as much as I have!

—Dan Harper
January, 2014
San Mateo, California

1. Angels We Have Heard on High (1st)

v. 1, French carol, trans. James Chadwick; vv. 2-3, Anon.

French carol melody, arr. Edward S. Barnes, c. 1915

1. An-gels we have heard on high Sweet-ly sing-ing o'er the plains
And the mountains in re-ply E-cho-ing their joy-ous strains.

2. In the fields be-side their sheep, Shepherds watching thro' the night,
Hear, a-mid the si-lence deep, Those sweet voic-es, clear and bright.

3. Joy-ful hearts with one ac-cord, Spread the ti-dings far and wide;
Born to us is Christ the Lord, At this hap-py Christ-mas tide.

Glo - - - - - - ri-a, in ex-cel-sis De - o, De - o.

ANGEL VOICES. 7.7.7.7. WITH REFRAIN

THE YULETIDE SONG AND CAROL BOOK © 2014 DAN HARPER

2. Angels We Have Heard on High (2nd)

French carol,
Trans. James Chadwick, 1860

French carol melody,
arr. Edward S. Barnes, c. 1915

1. An-gels we have heard on high / Sweet-ly sing-ing o'er the plains, / And the moun-tains in re-ply / E-cho-ing their joy-ous strains.
2. Shep-herds, why this ju-bi-lee? / Why your joy-ous strains pro-long? / What the glad-some tid-ings be / Which in-spire your heav'n-ly song?
3. Come to Beth-le-hem and see / Him whose birth the an-gels sing; / Come, a-dore on bend-ed knee, / Christ the Lord, the new-born king.
4. See him in a man-ger laid, / Whom the choirs of an-gels praise; / Ma-ry, Jo-seph, lend your aid, / While our hearts in love we raise.

Glo- - - - - - - - - ri-a,

ANGEL VOICES. 7.7.7.7. WITH REFRAIN

ANGELS WE HAVE HEARD ON HIGH (2)

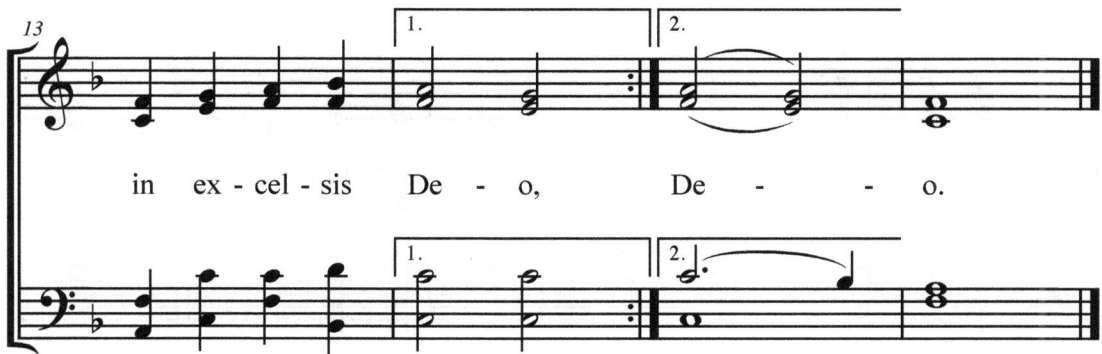

in ex - cel - sis De - o, De - o.

The 18th century French carol:

1. Les anges dans nos campagnes
Ont entonné l'hymne des cieux;
Et l'écho de nos montagnes
Redit ce chant mélodieux.
    Gloria, in excelsis Deo,
    Gloria, in excelsis Deo.

2. Bergers, pour qui cette fête?
Quel est l'objet de tous ces chants?
Quel vainqueur, quelle conquête
Mérite ces cris triomphants?
    Gloria, in excelsis Deo,
    Gloria, in excelsis Deo.

3. Ils annoncent la naissance
Du libérateur d'Israël,
Et pleins de reconnaissance
Chantent en ce jour solennel.
    Gloria, in excelsis Deo,
    Gloria, in excelsis Deo.

4. Bergers, loin de vos retraites
Unissez-vous à leurs concerts
Et que vos tendres musettes
Fassent retentir dans les airs:
    Gloria, in excelsis Deo,
    Gloria, in excelsis Deo.

5. Cherchons tous l'heureux village
Qui l'a vu naître sous ses toits,
Offrons-lui le tendre hommage
Et de nos coeurs et de nos voix!
    Gloria, in excelsis Deo,
    Gloria, in excelsis Deo.

3. Away in a Manger

Anonymous; prob. 19th century American

James R. Murry, *Royal Praise for the Sunday School,* 1888

1. A-way in a man-ger, No crib for a bed. The lit-tle Lord Je-sus Lay down his sweet head. The stars in the sky Looked down where he lay, The lit-tle Lord Je-sus A-sleep in the hay, The lit-tle Lord Je-sus A-sleep on the hay.

2. The cat-tle are low-ing, The poor ba-by wakes, But lit-tle Lord Je-sus, No cry-ing he makes. I love thee, Lord Je-sus: Look down from the sky, And stay by my crib Watch-ing lu-la-by, And stay by my crib, Watch-ing lu-la-by.

This text from May 3, 1884, issue of *The Myrtle*, Universalist Publishing House, Boston.

MUELLER. 6.5.6.5.6.5.6.5.6.5.6.5.

THE YULETIDE SONG AND CAROL BOOK © 2014 DAN HARPER

4. Boar's Head Carol

Traditional, Queens College, Oxford

1. The boar's head in hand bear I, Bedeck'd with bays and rosemary, And I pray you, my masters, be merry: Quot estis in convivio.
2. The boar's head as I understand, Is the rarest dish in all this land, Which thus bedecked with a gay garland Let us servire contico,
3. Our steward hath provided this In honor of the King of bliss, Which on this day to be servéd is, In reginensi atrio.

Caput Apri defero Reddens laudes Domino.

The Latin phrases may be replaced with the following:
"Quot estis in convivio" — As you all feast so heartily.
"...servire contico" — ...serve with a song merry.
"In reginensi atrio" — In the Queen's hall where we shall be.
"Caput apri defero reddens laudes Domino" —
　Lo, the head I bring to ye, / Now praise God full cheerfully.

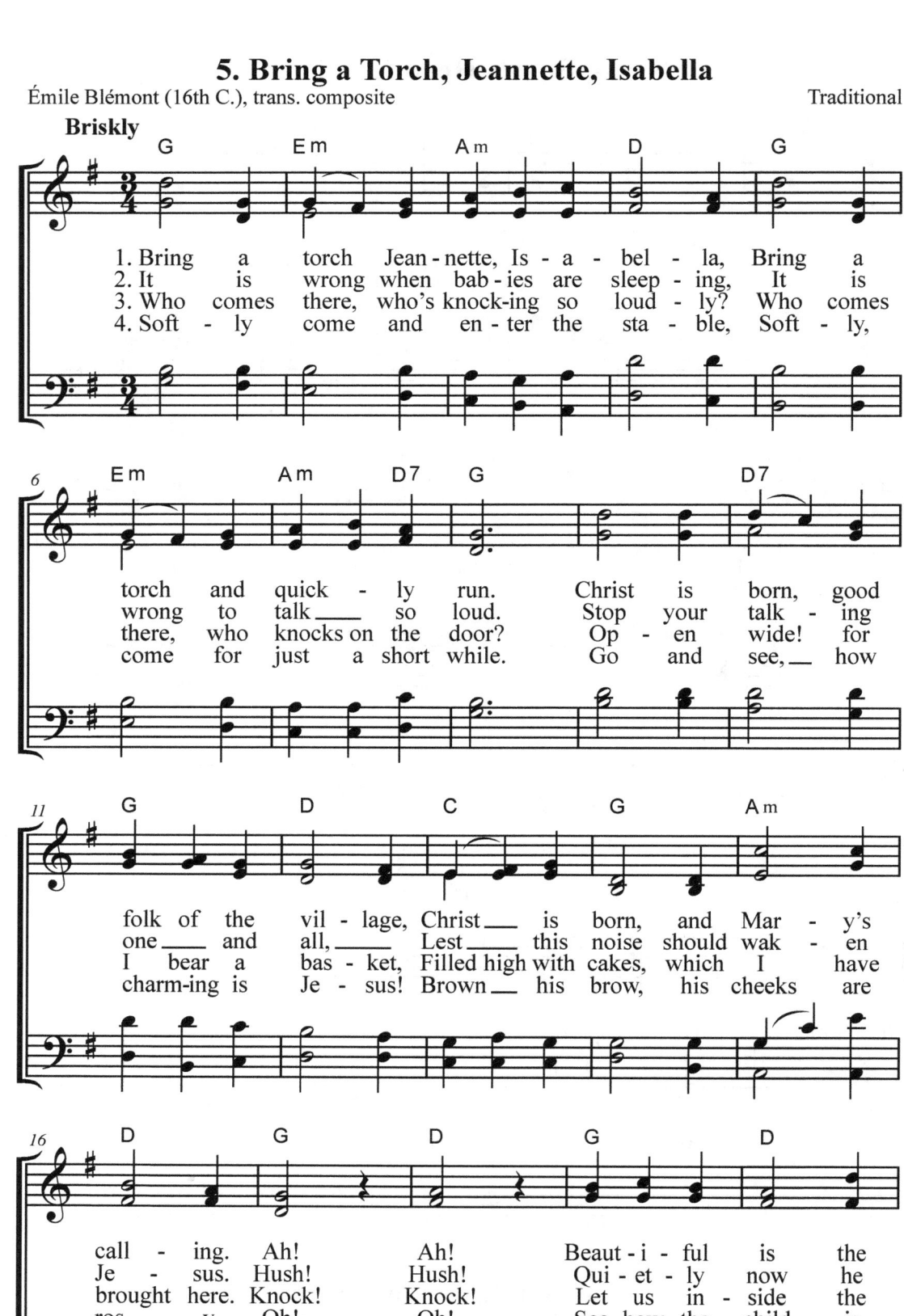

BRING A TORCH JEANNETTE, ISABELLA

moth - er, Ah! Ah! Beaut-i-ful is her child.
slum - bers, Hush! Hush! Qui - et - ly now he sleeps.
sta - ble! Knock! Knock! So we can cel - e - brate.
sleep - ing, Oh! Oh! See how he smiles and dreams.

1. Un flambeau, Jeanette, Isabelle,
Un flambeau, courons au berceau.
C'est Jésus, bonnes gens du hameau,
Le Christ est né, Marie appelle:
Ah! Ah! Ah! Que la mère est belle,
Ah! Ah! Ah! Que l'enfant est beau.

2. C'est un tort quand l'enfant someille,
C'est un tort de crier si fort.
Taisez-vous l'un et l'autre d'abord!
Au moindre bruit Jésus s'éville.
Chut! Chut! Chut! Il dort à merveille!
Chut! Chut! Chut! Ivoyez comme il dort.

3. Qui vient là, frappant de la sorte?
Qui vient là, frappant comme ça?
Ouvrez donc! J'ai posé sur un plat
De bons gâteaux qu'ici j'apporte.
Toc! Toc! Toc! Ouvrez-nous la porte!
Toc! Toc! Toc! Faisons grand gala!

4. Doucement dans l'étable close,
Doucement venez un moment.
Approchez, que Jésus est charmant!
Comme il est brun, comme il est rose!
Do! Do! Do! que l'enfant repose!
Do! Do! Do! qu'il rit en dormant.

A Child This Day Is Born

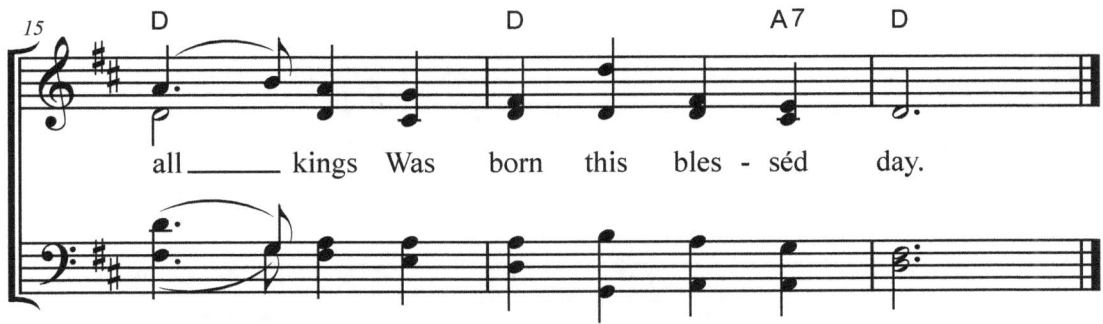

6. Now such a place it was
Where this was come to pass
For want of room this child was laid
Betwixt an ox and ass.

Refrain.

7. Not sumptuously, but simply
Was this young king arrayed,
A manger was the cradle
Where this young child was laid.

Refrain.

7. Children, Go Where I Send Thee

from a Library of Congress recording, 1942

Trad. African American

1. One was the little bitty baby…
2. Two was the Paul and Silas…
3. Three was the Hebrew children…
4. Four was the four come knocking at the door…
5. Five was the gospel writers…
6. Six was the six that couldn't get fixed…
7. Seven was the seven who went to heaven…
8. Eight was the eight that stood at the gate…
9. Nine was the nine that looked so fine…
10. Ten was the ten commandments…
11. Eleven was the eleven deriders…
12. Twelve was the twelve disciples…

8. Cornish Wassail

Traditional / Traditional

1. Now Christmas is comen and New Year begin, Pray open your doors and let us come in.
2. O Master and Mistress sitting down by the fire While we poor wassail boys travel in the mire.
3. This ancient house we will kindly salute, It is an old custom you need not dispute.
4. We hope that your apple trees prosper and bear, And bring forth good cider when we come next year.
5. We hope that your barley will prosper and grow That you may have plenty and some to bestow.
6. Good Master and Mistress, how can you forbear? Come fill up our bowl with cider and beer.
7. We wish you a blessing and long time to live, Since you've been so free and wiling to give.

With our wassail, wassail, wassail, And joy come with our jolly wassail.

Can wasel. IRREGULAR   THE YULETIDE SONG AND CAROL BOOK © 2014 DAN HARPER

9. Coventry Carol

Attr. Robert Croo, 1534

Traditional, c.1591, arr.
Bramley and Stainer, 1878

1. Lu - lay, thou lit - tle ti - ny child, By, by, lu - ly, lul - lay: Lul - lay, thou lit - tle ti - ny child, By by, lu - ly, lul - lay.
2. O, sis - ters too, how may we do, For to pre - serve this day, This poor young - ling for whom we sing, By, by, lu - ly, lul - lay?
3. Her - od the king in his rag - ing, Charg - éd he hath this day His men of might, in his own sight, All chil - dren young to slay.
4. Then woe is me, poor child, for thee, And ev - er mourn and say, For thy part - ing nor say nor sing, By, by, lul - ly, lul - lay.

COVENTRY CAROL. C.M.

THE YULETIDE SONG AND CAROL BOOK © 2014 DAN HARPER

THE CUTTY WREN

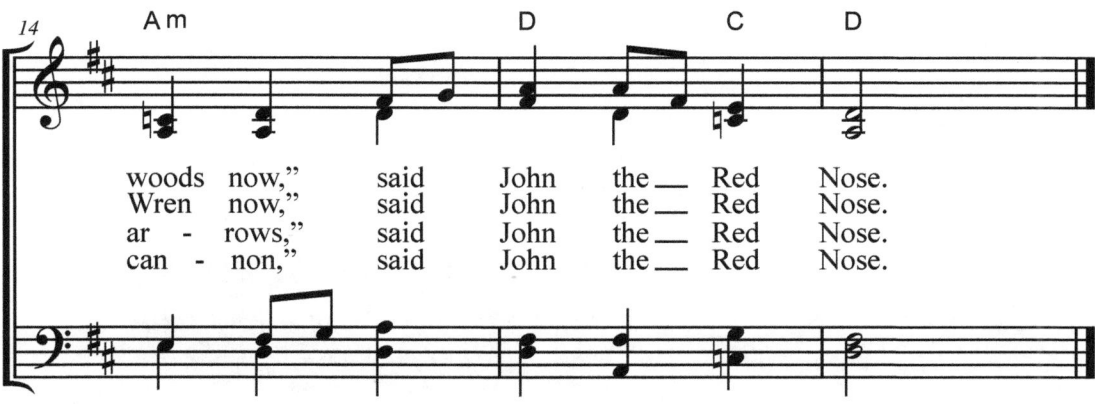

woods now," said John the — Red Nose.
Wren now," said John the — Red Nose.
ar - rows," said John the — Red Nose.
can - non," said John the — Red Nose.

5. "O, how will you bring her home?" said Millder to Malder;
"O, I cannot tell you," said Festel to Fose;
"On four strong men's shoulders," said John the Red Nose…

6. "O, that will not do," said Millder to Malder;
"O, what will do then?" said Festel to Fose;
"In carts and in waggons," said John the Red Nose…

7. "O, how will you carve her?" said Millder to Malder;
"O, I cannot tell you," said Festel to Fose;
"With knives and with forks," said John the Red Nose…

8. "O, that will not do," said Millder to Malder;
"O, what will do then?" said Festel to Fose;
"With hatchets and cleavers," said John the Red Nose…

9. "O, how will you boil her?" said Millder to Malder;
"O, I cannot tell you," said Festel to Fose;
"In pots and in kettles," said John the Red Nose…

10. "O, that will not do," said Millder to Malder;
"O, what will do then?" said Festel to Fose;
"In pans and in cauldrons," said John the Red Nose…

11. "O, who'll get the spare ribs? said Millder to Malder;
"O, I cannot tell you," said Festel to Fose;
"We'll give them to the poor," said John the Red Nose…

Miss Mason states that she learned this song from her Welsh nurses, adding: "It was an ancient custom in South Wales for two or four men to go about on St. Stephen's Day carrying a wren fastened on two poles slung on their shoulders, groaning under its supposed weight, and singing this song." While Miss Mason gives a different tune for this song, this tune is more familiar.

Richard Davis? c.1920

13. The Friendly Beasts (1st)

Pierre de Corbeil, d. 1222,
altered—harm. anonymous

1. Jesus, our brother, strong and good, Was humbly born in a stable rude, And the friendly beasts around him stood, Jesus, our brother, strong and good.
2. "I," said the donkey, shaggy and brown, "I carried his mother uphill and down, I carried his mother to Bethlehem town, I," said the donkey shaggy and brown.
3. "I," said the cow, all white and red, "I gave him my manger for his bed, I gave him hay to pillow his head, I," said the cow, all white and red.
4. "I," said the sheep with curly horn, "I gave him my wool for his blanket warm, He wore my coat on Christmas morn, I," said the sheep with curly horn.
5. "I," said the dove, from the rafters high, "I cooed him to sleep that he should not cry, We cooed him to sleep, my mate and I; I," said the dove from the rafters high.
6. Thus all the beasts, by some good spell, in the stable dark were glad to tell, Of the gifts they gave Emmanuel, The gifts they gave Emmanuel.

ORIENTIS PARTIBUS (ALT.). IRREGULAR (L.M.) THE YULETIDE SONG AND CAROL BOOK © 2014 DAN HARPER

Some of the many additional verses which have been added to this carol by unknown authors:

7. "I," said the sheepdog, black and white,
"I guarded the child through darkest night,
"I watched o'er him till morning light,
"I," said the sheepdog, black and white.

8. "I," said the cat with warm gray fur,
"I sang him to sleep with my soft purr,
"I sang to him so he would not stir,
"I," said the cat with warm gray fur.

9. "I," said the camel, traveler bold,
"I followed the star that was foretold,
"I brought him gifts of spices and gold,
"I," said the camel, traveler bold.

10. "I," said the mouse, "the poorest of you,
"I offered to him my love most true,
"This was the greatest gift that he knew,
"I," said the mouse, "the poorest of you."

15. Gaudete

Piae Cantiones

♩ = c.120 *Refrain:*

Piae Cantiones, 1582 (refrain);
Jistebnice Cantional, 1420 (verses)

Gau-de-te! Gau-de-te! Christus est na-tus
Ex Ma-ri-a Vir-gi-ne: gau-de-te!

Verses (Solo):

1. Tem-pus ad-est gra-ti-æ Hoc quod op-ta-ba-mus;
2. Er-go nos-tra con-ci-o Psal-lat jam in lus-tro;

Car-mi-na lae-ti-ci-æ De-vo-te red-da-mus.
Be-ne-di-cat Do-mi-no: Sal-us Re-gi nos-tro.

Verses may be sung in soprano, alto/tenor, or bass ranges.

Refrain: O, rejoice! O, rejoice! for Christ is born—
Of Mary, the virgin pure, O, rejoice!

1. Lo, the time of grace has come,
That for which we prayed long;
Let us sing of our great joy,
Let us sing devout songs.

2. Therefore our assembly shall
Come together and sing
Praise to God, and also greet
Christ, who shall be our King.

GAUDETE. 11.10. WITH REFRAIN

Go Tell It on the Mountains

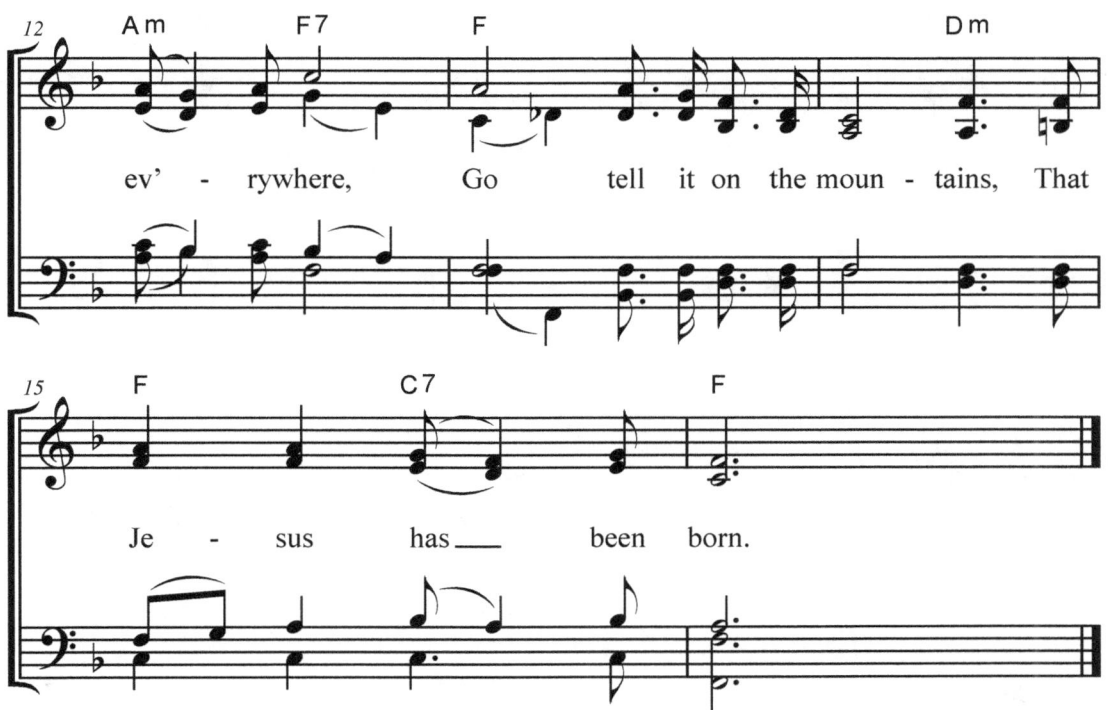

2

17. God Rest Ye Merry, Gentlemen (1st)

Traditional words

Traditional tune
arr. Bramley and Stainer c. 1860

1. God rest ye mer-ry, gen-tle-men, let noth-ing you dis-may, Re-mem-ber Christ our sav-ior was born on Christ-mas day, To save us all from Sat-an's power when we had gone a-stray,
2. In Beth-le-hem, in Is-ra-el, this bles-sed babe was born, And laid with-in a man-ger u-pon this bles-sed morn, The which his mo-ther Mar-y did no-thing take in scorn, O,
3. From God our heav'n-ly fa-ther, a bles-sed an-gel came And un-to cer-tain shep-herds brought tid-ings of the same, How that in Beth-le-hem was born the son of God by name,

GOD REST YE MERRY. 8.6.8.6.8.6. WITH REFRAIN THE YULETIDE SONG AND CAROL BOOK © 2014 DAN HARPER

GOD REST YE MERRY, GENTLEMEN (1ST)

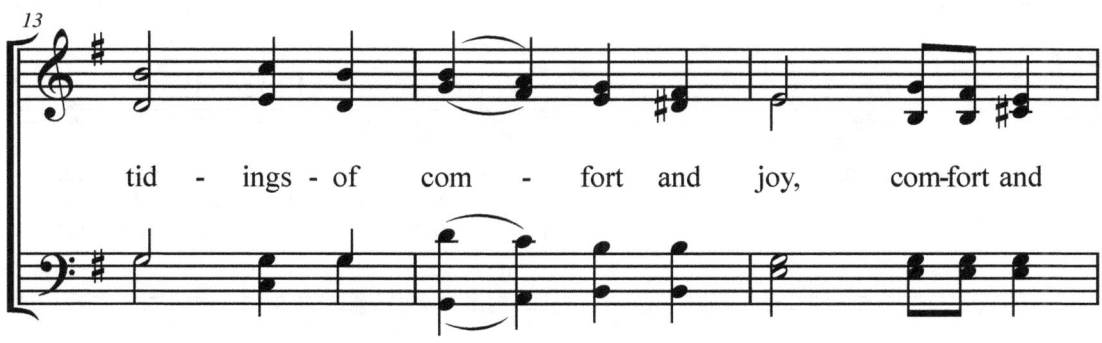

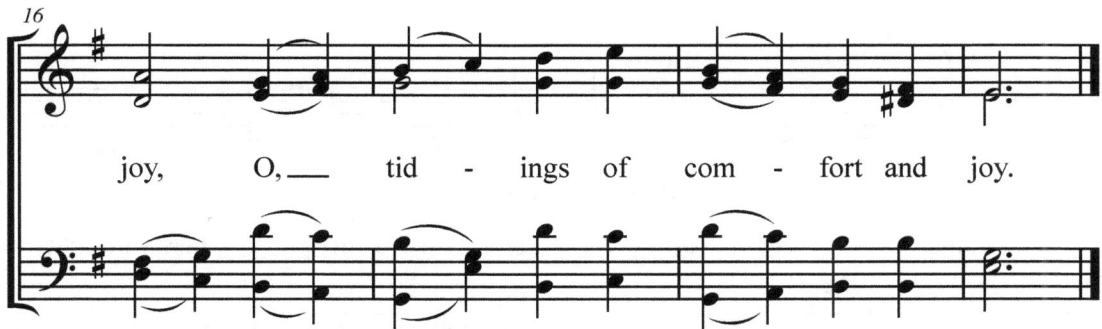

4. "Fear not," then said the Angel,
"Let nothing you affright,
This day is born a savior
Of a pure virgin bright,
To free all those who trust in him
From Satan's power and might."
Refrain.

5. The shepherds at those tidings
Rejoicéd much in mind,
And left their flocks a-feeding
In tempest, storm and wind,
And went to Bethlehem straightway
This blessed babe to find.
Refrain.

6. But when to Bethlehem they came,
Whereas this infant lay,
They found him in a manger,
Where oxen feed on hay;
His mother Mary kneeling,
Unto the Lord did pray:
Refrain.

7. With sudden joy and gladness
The shepherds were beguiled,
To see the babe of Israel
Before his mother mild,
O then with joy and cheerfulness
Rejoice, each mother's child,
Refrain.

8. Now to the Lord sing praises,
All you within this place,
And with true love and brotherhood
Each other now embrace;
This holy tide of Christmas
All other doth deface.
Refrain.

9. God bless the ruler of this house
And send him long to reign,
And many a merry Christmas
May live to see again,
Among your friends and kindred
That live both far and near
    That God send you a happy new year,
    Happy new year,
    That God send you a happy new year.

18. God Rest Ye Merry, Gentlemen (2nd)

Traditional words

Trad., arranged Rimbault (1846)

1. God rest ye mer-ry, gen-tle-men, let noth-ing you dis-may, Re-mem-ber Christ our sav-ior was born on Christ-mas day, To save us all from Sat-an's power when we were gone a-stray, O,___
2. In Beth-le-hem, in Is-ra-el, this bles-sed babe was born, And laid with-in a man-ger u-pon this bles-sed morn, The which his mo-ther Mar-y did no-thing take in scorn, O,___
3. From God our heav'n-ly fa-ther, a bles-sed an-gel came And un-to cer-tain shep-herds brought tid-ings of the same, How that in Beth-le-hem was born the son of God by name,

RIMBAULT. 8.6.8.6.8.6. WITH REFRAIN

THE YULETIDE SONG AND CAROL BOOK © 2014 DAN HARPER

GOD REST YE MERRY, GENTLEMEN (2ND)

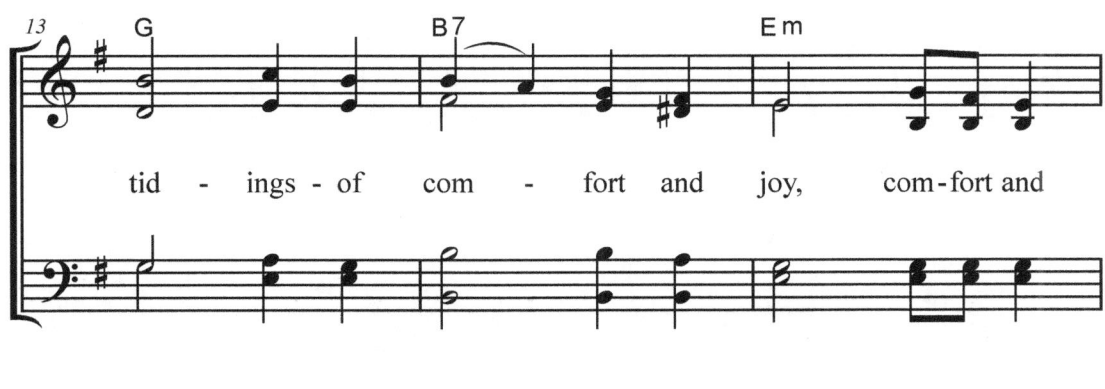

4. "Fear not," then said the Angel,
"Let nothing you affright,
This day is born a savior
Of a pure virgin bright,
To free all those who trust in him
From Satan's power and might."
   Refrain.

5. The shepherds at those tidings
Rejoicéd much in mind,
And left their flocks a-feeding
In tempest, storm and wind,
And went to Bethlehem straightway
This blessed babe to find.
   Refrain.

6. But when to Bethlehem they came,
Whereas this infant lay,
They found him in a manger,
Where oxen feed on hay;
His mother Mary kneeling,
Unto the Lord did pray:
   Refrain.

7. With sudden joy and gladness
The shepherds were beguiled,
To see the babe of Israel
Before his mother mild,
O then with joy and cheerfulness
Rejoice, each mother's child,
   Refrain.

8. Now to the Lord sing praises,
All you within this place,
And with true love and brotherhood
Each other now embrace;
This holy tide of Christmas
All other doth deface.
   Refrain.

9. God bless the ruler of this house
And send him long to reign,
And many a merry Christmas
May live to see again,
Among your friends and kindred
That live both far and near
   That God send you a happy new year,
   Happy new year,
   That God send you a happy new year.

19. Good Christian Men, Rejoice

Trans. John M. Neale, 1853, alt.
Michael Prætorius
Harm. John Stainer, 1867

*or "folk"

1. Good Christian men,* rejoice With heart, and soul, and voice; Give ye heed to what we say: News! News! Jesus Christ is born to-day: Ox and ass before him bow, And he is in the manger now. Christ is born to-day! Christ is born to-day!

2. Good Christian men,* rejoice, With heart, and soul, and voice; Tidings hear of fullest bliss: Joy! Joy! Jesus Christ was born for this: Unto you both way and door— And life and light forevermore. Christ was born for this! Christ was born for this!

IN DUCLI JUBILO 6.6.7.2.7.7.8.5.5.

THE YULETIDE SONG AND CAROL BOOK © 2014 DAN HARPER

John Mason Neale, 1853 **20. Good King Wenceslas** *Piae Cantiones*, 1582
Arr. Henry Bramley & John Stainer, 1871

1. Good King Wen-ces-las looked out, on the feast of Ste-phen, When the snow lay round a-bout, deep and crisp and ev-en: Bright-ly shone the moon that night, though the frost was cru-el,
2. "Hith-er page, and stand by me, if thou know-est, tel-ling: Yon-der pea-sant, who is he? where and what his dwel-ling?" "Sire he lives a good league hence, un-der-neath the moun-tain,
3. "Bring me flesh, and bring me wine, bring me pine-logs hith-er. Thou and I will see him dine when we bear them thith-er." Page and mon-arch, forth they went, forth they went to-geth-er,
4. "Sire, the night is dark-er now, and the wind blows strong-er; Fails my heart, I know not how; I can go no long-er." "Mark my foot-steps, good my page, tread thou in them bold-ly;
5. In his mas-ter's steps he trod, where the snow lay din-ted; Heat was in the ver-y sod which the saint hath print-ed. There-fore, gen-tle-folk, be sure, wealth or rank pos-ses-sing,

TEMPUS ADEST FLORIDUM. 7.6.7.6.7.6.7.6.   THE YULETIDE SONG AND CAROL BOOK © 2014 DAN HARPER

GOOD KING WENCESLAS

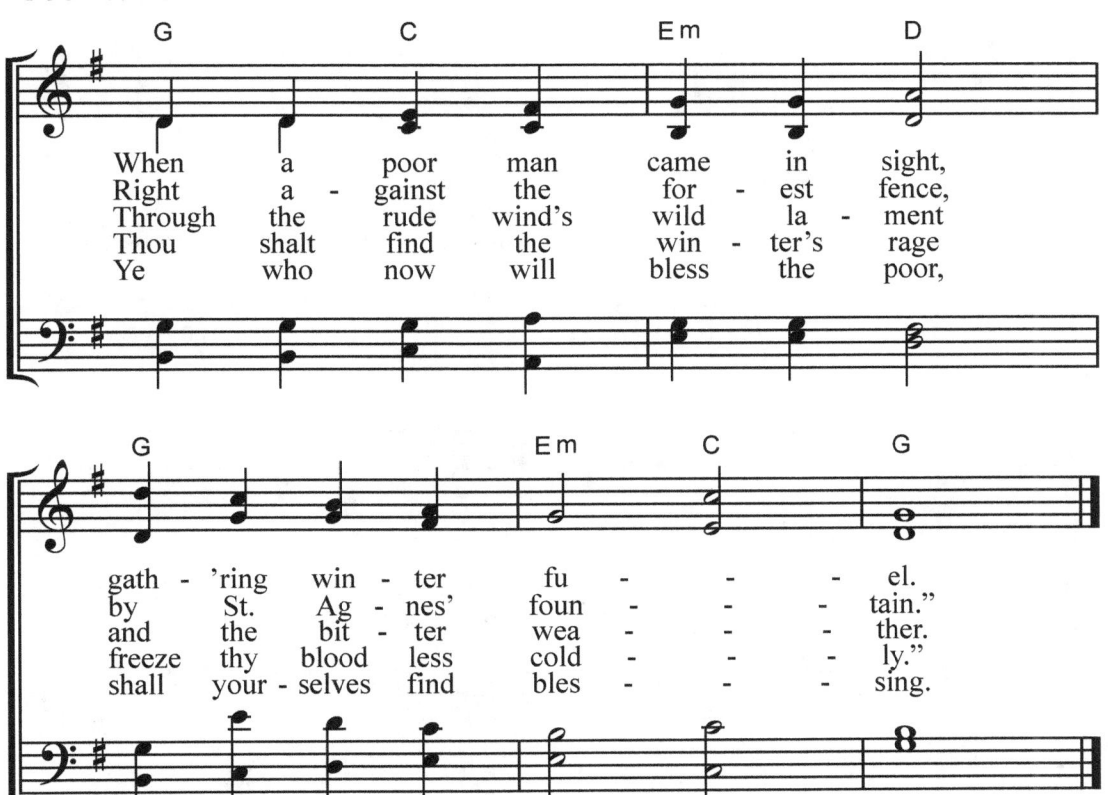

23. I Heard the Bells on Christmas Day (1st)

Henry W. Longfellow

Traditional, arr.
Ralph Vaughan Williams, 1906

1. I heard the bells on Christ - mas day, Their
2. And in des - pair I bowed my head; "There
3. Then pealed the bells more loud and deep: "God

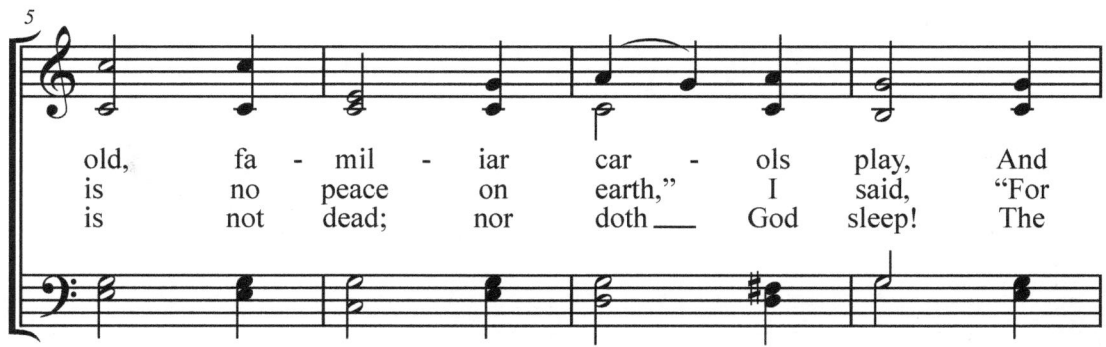
old, fa - mil - iar car - ols play, And
is no peace on earth," I said, "For
is not dead; nor doth God sleep! The

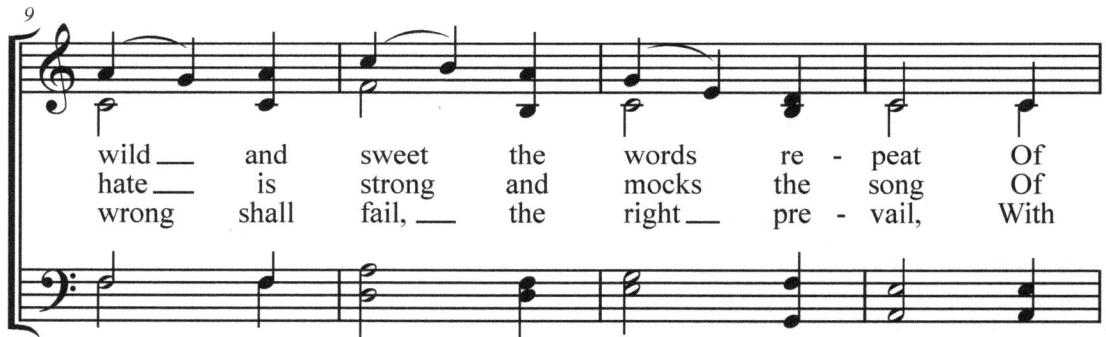
wild and sweet the words re - peat Of
hate is strong and mocks the song Of
wrong shall fail, the right pre - vail, With

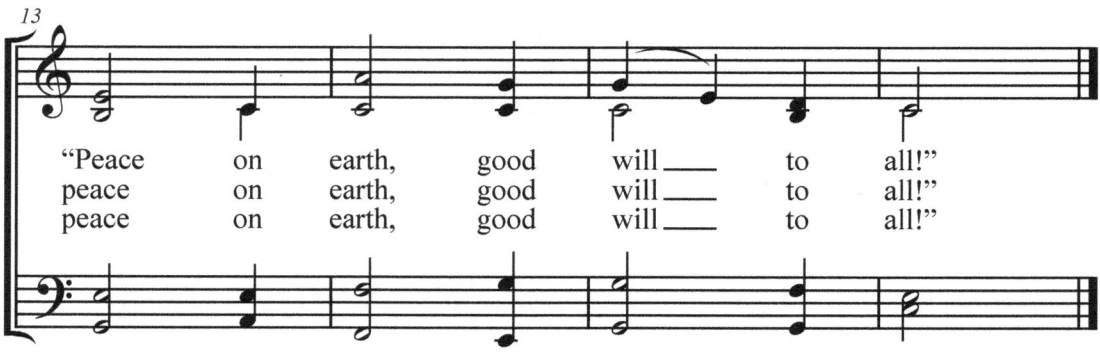
"Peace on earth, good will to all!"
peace on earth, good will to all!"
peace on earth, good will to all!"

HERONGATE. L.M.   THE YULETIDE SONG AND CAROL BOOK © 2014 DAN HARPER

24. I Heard the Bells on Christmas Day (2nd)

Henry W. Longfellow *Genevan Psalter, 1550*

1. I heard the bells on Christmas day, Their old, familiar carols play, And wild and sweet the words repeat Of "Peace on earth, good will to all!"
2. And ringing, singing, on its way, The world revolved from night to day, A voice, a chime, a chant sublime, Of "Peace on earth, good will to all!"

OLD HUNDREDTH. L.M.

26. It Came upon the Midnight Clear

Edmund H. Sears, 1849 — Richard S. Willis, 1850

1. It came up-on the mid-night clear, That glo-rious song of old, From an-gels bend-ing near the earth, To touch their harps of gold: "Peace on the earth, good-will to men, From heaven's all-gra-cious king." The
2. Still thro' the clo-ven skies they come, With peace-ful wings un-furled; And still their heaven-ly mu-sic floats O'er all the wea-ry world. A-bove its sad and low-ly plains They bend on hov-ering wing; And
3. But with the woes of sin and strife The world has suf-fered long; Be-neath the an-gel-strain have rolled Two thou-sand years of wrong; And man, at war with man, hears not The love song which they bring. O
4. For, lo! the days are has-tening on By pro-phet bards fore-told, When with the ev-er-cir-cling years Comes round the age of gold: When peace shall o-ver all the earth Its an-cient splen-dors fling, And

CAROL. C.M.D. — THE YULETIDE SONG AND CAROL BOOK © 2014 DAN HARPER

It Came upon the Midnight Clear

2

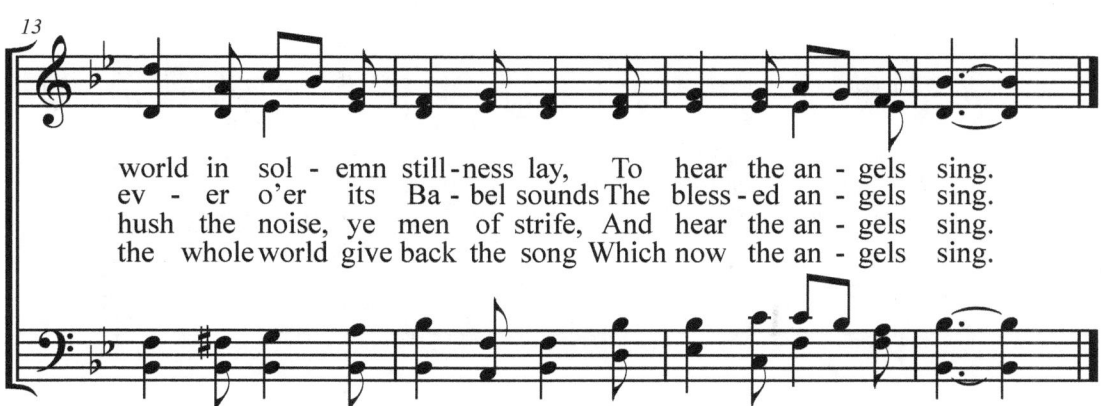

world in sol - emn still-ness lay, To hear the an - gels sing.
ev - er o'er its Ba - bel sounds The bless - ed an - gels sing.
hush the noise, ye men of strife, And hear the an - gels sing.
the whole world give back the song Which now the an - gels sing.

27. Jingle Bells

James Pierpont
James Pierpont

1. Dash-ing through the snow, In a one horse o-pen sleigh, O'er the fields we go, Laugh-ing all the way. Bells on bob-tail ring, Mak-ing spir-its bright, What fun it is to ride and sing A sleigh-ing song to-night,
2. A day or two a-go I thought I'd take a ride, And soon Miss Fan-ny Bright, Was seat-ed by my side. The horse was lean and lank, Mis-for-tune seemed his lot, He got in-to a drift-ed bank, And there we got up-sot.
3. Now the ground is white, Go it while you're young, Take the girls to-night, And sing this sleigh-ing song, Just get a bob-tail nag, Two-for-ty for his speed, And hitch him to an o-pen sleigh, And crack! you'll take the lead.

PIERPONT. IRREGULAR (6.6.6.6.6.6.8.6. W/REFRAIN) THE YULETIDE SONG AND CAROL BOOK © 2014 DAN HARPER

JINGLE BELLS

JOY TO THE WORLD

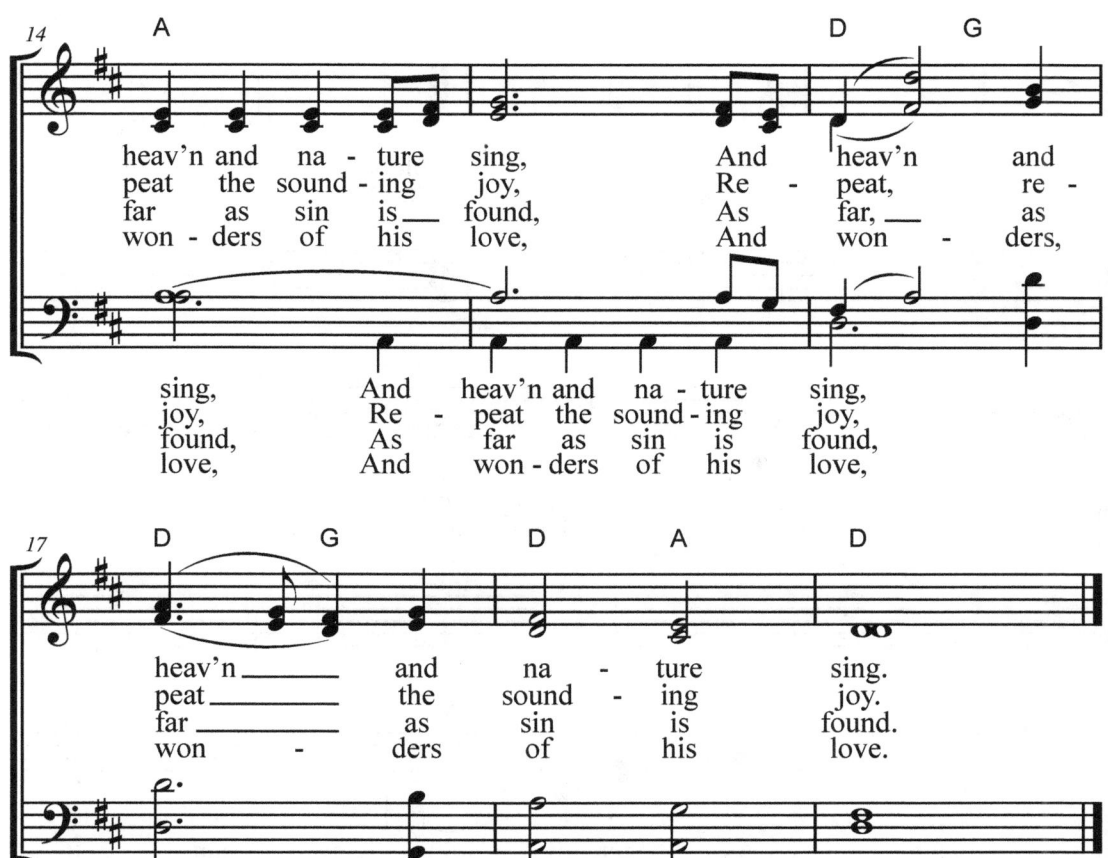

30. Lo, How a Rose E'er Blooming

Conrad Mainz? c.1558,
trans. Theodore Baker, 1894

Anon. 16th century,
arr. Michael Praetorius, 1609

1. Lo, how a Rose e'er bloom-ing From tender stem hath sprung, Of Jesse's lineage com-ing As men of old have sung. It came, a flow-ret bright, A-mid the cold of winter, When half-spent was the night.
2. I-saiah 'twas fore-told it, The Rose I have in mind; With Ma-ry we be-hold it, The vir-gin moth-er kind. To show God's love a-right, She bore to us a sav-ior, When half-spent was the night.

ES IST EIN' ROS' ENTSPRUNGEN. 7.6.7.6.6.7.6. THE YULETIDE SONG AND CAROL BOOK © 2014 DAN HARPER

31. Mary Had a Baby

1. Mary had a baby, oh, Lord,
Mary had a baby, oh, my Lord,
Mary had a baby, oh, Lord,
   Refrain: The people keep a-coming,
   and the train done gone.

2. What did she name him?…

3. She called him Jesus…

4. Where was he born?…

5. Born into a stable…

6. Where did they lay him?…

7. Laid him in a manger…

8. Star it shined above him…

9. Shepherds knelt before him…

10. Wise men brought him presents…

11. Herod tried to find them…

12. So they fled to Egypt…

13. Angel flew above them…

John F. Wade, c. 1743
Trans. Frederick Oakeley, 1852

32. O Come, All Ye Faithful

John F. Wade, c. 1743

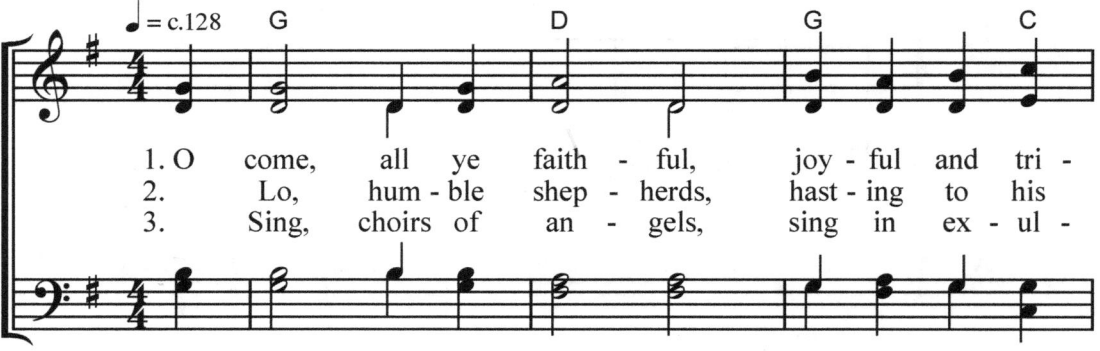
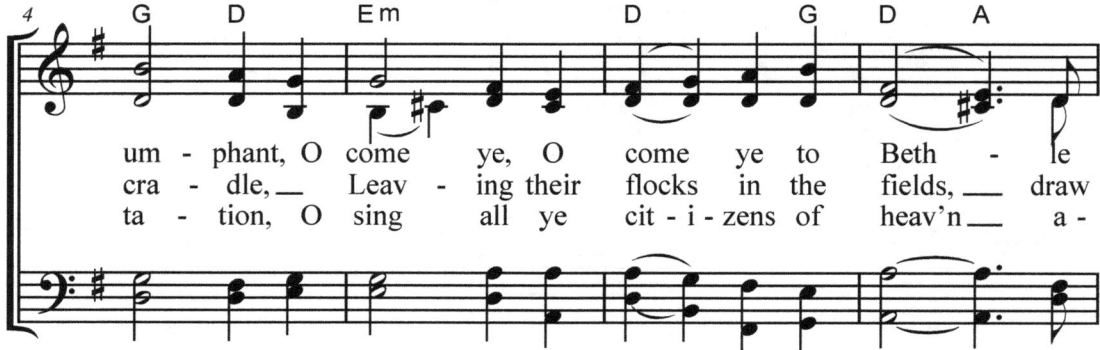
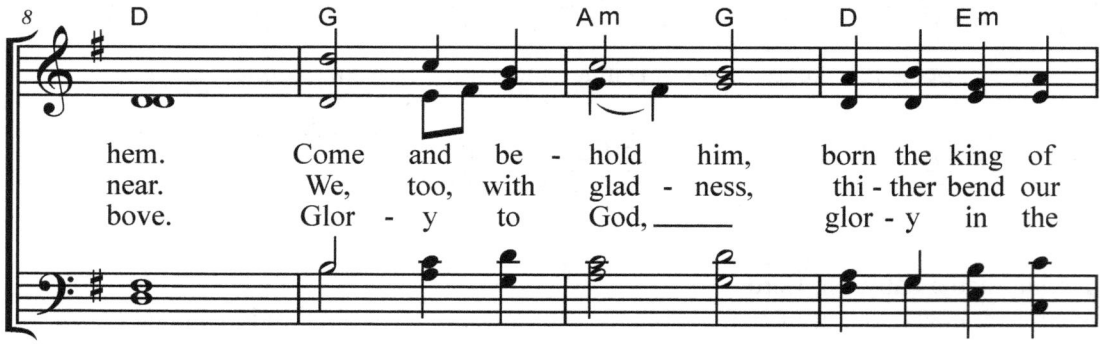
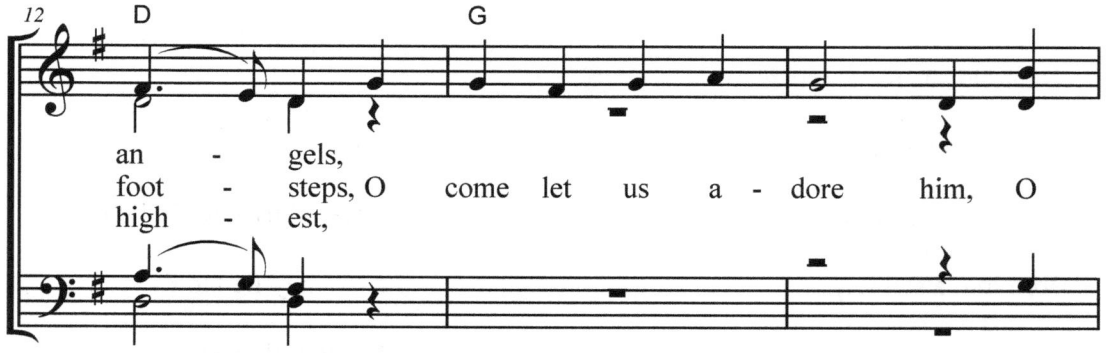

ADESTES FIDELES. 12.11.11. WITH REFRAIN

THE YULETIDE SONG AND CAROL BOOK © 2014 DAN HARPER

O Come All Ye Faithful

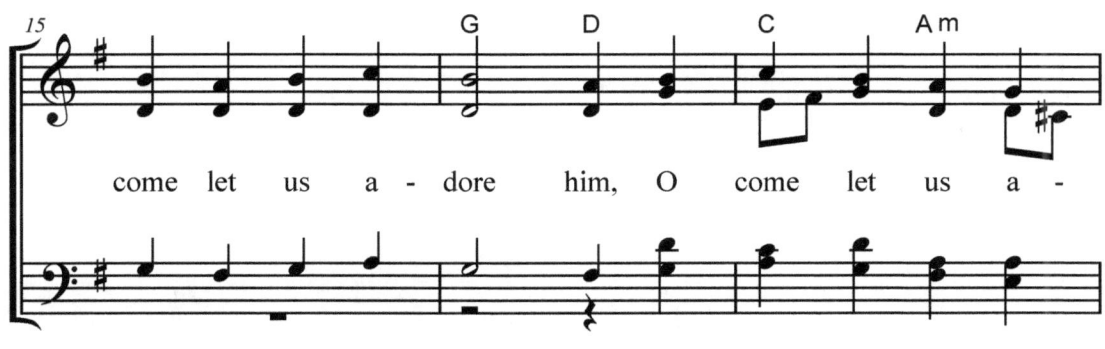

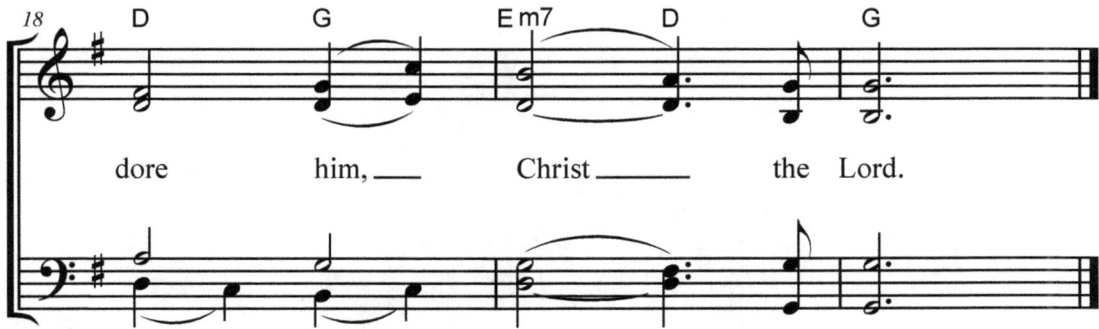

1. Adeste fideles læti triumphantes,
Venite, venite in Bethlehem.
Natum videte
Regem angelorum:

   Refrain: Venite adoremus,
   Venite adoremus,
   Venite adoremus,
   Dominum.

2. Deum de Deo, lumen de lumine
Gestant puellæ viscera.
Deum verum, genitum non factum.
   Refrain.

3. Cantet nunc 'Io,' chorus angelorum;
Cantet nunc aula cælestium,
Gloria! Soli Deo Gloria!
   Refrain.

34. O Little Town of Bethlehem (1st)

Phillips Brooks, 1868
Trad. English melody, arr. Ralph Vaughan Williams, 1906

♩ = c.108

1. O little town of Bethlehem, How still we see thee lie! Above thy deep and dreamless sleep, The silent stars go by: Yet in thy dark streets shineth The
2. For Christ is born of Mary, And gathered all above, While mortals sleep, the angels keep Their watch of wond'ring love. O, morning stars together Pro-
3. How silently, how silently, The wondrous gift is giv'n! So God imparts to human hearts The blessings of his heav'n. No ear may hear his coming, But

FOREST GREEN. 8.6.8.6.7.6.8.6. THE YULETIDE SONG AND CAROL BOOK © 2014 DAN HARPER

O LITTLE TOWN OF BETHELEHEM (1ST)

35. O Little Town of Bethlehem (2nd)

Phillips Brooks, 1868 — Lewis Henry Redner, 1868

1. O little town of Bethlehem, How still we see thee lie! Above thy deep and dreamless sleep, The silent stars go by: Yet in thy dark streets shineth The
2. For Christ is born of Mary, And gathered all above, While mortals sleep, the angels keep Their watch of won-d'ring love. O, morning stars together Pro-
3. How silently, how silently, The wondrous gift is giv'n! So God imparts to human hearts The blessings of his heav'n. No ear may hear his coming, But

St. Louis. 8.6.8.6.7.6.8.6.   THE YULETIDE SONG AND CAROL BOOK © 2014 DAN HARPER

O Little Town of Bethelehem (2nd)

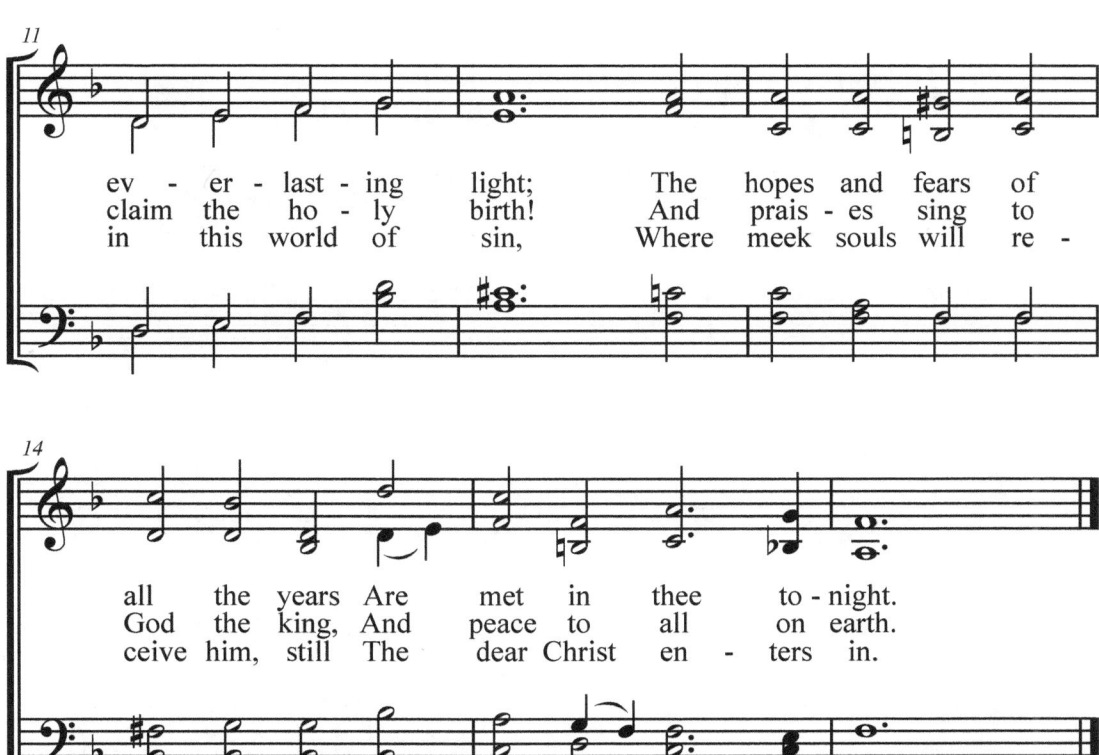

O TANNENBAUM

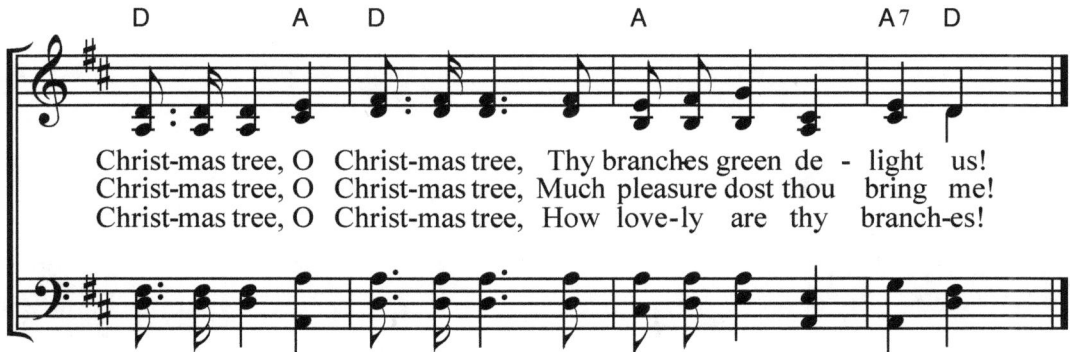

1. O Tannenbaum, O Tannenbaum,
Wie grün sind deine Blätter!
Du grünst nicht nur zur Sommerzeit,
Nein, auch im Winter, wenn es schneit.
O Tannenbaum, O Tannenbaum,
Wie grün sind deine Blätter!

2. O Tannenbaum, O Tannenbaum,
Du kannst mir sehr gefallen!
Wie oft hat schon zur Winterzeit
Ein Baum von dir mich hoch erfreut!
O Tannenbaum, O Tannenbaum,
Du kannst mir sehr gefallen!

3. O Tannenbaum, O Tannenbaum,
Dein Kleid will mich was lehren:
Die Hoffnung und Beständigkeit
Gibt Mut und Kraft zu jeder Zeit!
O Tannenbaum, O Tannenbaum,
Dein Kleid will mich was lehren!

37. Once in Royal David's City

Cecil Frances Alexander, 1848

Henry John Gaunlett, 1849
harm. Arthur H. Mann, 1919

1. Once in royal David's city Stood a lowly cattle shed, Where a mother laid her baby, In a manger for his bed. Mary was that mother mild, Jesus was her little child.
2. Jesus, born on Christmas morning, Blessed by God, the Lord of all, And his shelter was a stable, And his cradle was a stall; With the poor, oppress'd and lowly, He will live his life so holy.

Irby. 8.7.8.7.7.7.

THE YULETIDE SONG AND CAROL BOOK © 2014 DAN HARPER

THE PILGRIMS

To only tell the story of the pilgrims, end the song here.

1. En nombre del cielo,
Os pido posada,
Pues no puede andar
Ya mi esposa amada.

2. Aqui no es mesón
Sigan adelante
Pues no vaya a ser
Alguntunante.

3. Mi esposa es María
La Reina del Cielo
Os pido posada
Por solo una noche.

4. Pues si es una Reina
Quién lo solicita,
¿Cómo es que de noche
Anda tan solita?

5. Yo soy carpintero
De nombre José
Mi esposa es María
La Madre de Dios.

6. Si eres tu José
Y tu esposa es María
Entren, peregrinos,
No los conocía.

Part II:

1. Entren, santos peregrinos, peregrinos,
A este humilde rincón ;

2. No de mi pobre morada, morada,
Sino de mi corazón.

Part III:

1. Echen confites y canelones
Para los muchachos que son comelones.

2. Andale, Lola, no te dilates
Con la canasta de los cacahuates.

3. En esta posada nos hemos chasqueado
Porque la dueña nada nos ha dado.

39. Rise Up, Shepherd, and Follow

Religious Folk Songs of the Negro, 1874

1. There's a star in the East on Christmas morn; Rise up, shepherd, and follow! It will lead to the place where the Savior's born, Rise up, shepherd, and follow! Leave your ewes and leave your lambs, Rise up shepherd, and follow! Leave your sheep and leave your rams, Rise up, shepherd, and follow!

2. If you take good heed to the angel's words; Rise up, shepherd, and follow! You'll forget your flocks, you'll forget your herds, Rise up, shepherd, and follow!

To sing this as a call-and-response song:
– have a soloist sing two measures;
– have the chorus respond with two measures of "Rise up shepherd and follow";
– continue in this way until the end.

SHERBURNE

Changes from the original: transposed from G to E flat; tenor (melody) moved to soprano; treble moved to tenor; low E flats transposed up an octave in pickup measure, m. 1, m. 7.

STILLE NACHT
German words by Joseph Mohr, 1816

1. Stille Nacht! Heilige Nacht!
Alles schläft; einsam wacht
Nur das traute heilige Paar.
Holder Knab im lockigten Haar,
    Schlafe in himmlischer Ruh!
    Schlafe in himmlischer Ruh!

2. Stille Nacht! Heilige Nacht!
Gottes Sohn, o wie lacht
Lieb' aus deinem göttlichen Mund,
Da schlägt uns die rettende Stund.
    Jesus in deiner Geburt!
    Jesus in deiner Geburt!

3. Stille Nacht! Heilige Nacht!
Die der Welt Heil gebracht,
Aus des Himmels goldenen Höhn
Uns der Gnaden Fülle läßt sehn:
    Jesum in Menschengestalt,
    Jesum in Menschengestalt

4. Stille Nacht! Heilige Nacht!
Wo sich heut alle Macht
Väterlicher Liebe ergoß
Und als Bruder huldvoll umschloß
    Jesus die Völker der Welt,
    Jesus die Völker der Welt.

5. Stille Nacht! Heilige Nacht!
Lange schon uns bedacht,
Als der Herr vom Grimme befreit
In der Väter urgrauer Zeit
    Aller Welt Schonung verhieß,
    Welt Schonung verhieß.

6. Stille Nacht! Heilige Nacht!
Hirten erst kundgemacht
Durch der Engel Alleluja,
Tönt es laut bei Ferne und Nah:
    Jesus der Retter ist da!
    Jesus der Retter ist da!

44. Star in the East

Reginald Heber, 1811

All parts doubled an octave up or down.

Baptist Harmony, arr. William Walker, *Southern Harmony*, 1854

1. Hail, the blest morn, see the great Mediator, / Down from the regions of glory descend. / Shepherds, go worship the babe in the manger, / Lo, for his guard the bright angels attend.
2. Cold on this cradle the dewdrops are shining; / Low lies his bed, with the beasts of the stall; / Angels adore him in slumbers reclining, / Wise men and shepherds before him do fall.
3. Say, shall we yield him, in costly devotion, / Odors of Eden, and off'rings divine, / Gems from the mountains, and pearls from the ocean, / Myrrh from the forest, and gold from the mines.
4. Vainly we offer each ample oblation, / Vainly with gold we his favor secure, / Richer by far is the heart's adoration, / Dearest to God are the prayers of the poor.

STAR IN THE EAST. 11.10.11.10. WITH REFRAIN

THE YULETIDE SONG AND CAROL BOOK © 2014 DAN HARPER

STAR IN THE EAST 2

Notated by Walker as if in Aeolian mode, but may be sung in Dorian mode (with F♯).

45. Sussex Mummers Carol

Traditional English
Collected and arr. Lucy Broadwood, 1890

1. A glorious angel from heaven came Unto the virgin maid, Strange news and tidings of great joy The humble Mary had, The humble Mary had.
2. God bless the master of this house With happiness beside, Where-e'er his body rides or walks, His God must be his guide, His God must be his guide.
3. God bless the mistress of this house With gold chain round her breast, Where-e'er her body sleeps or wakes Lord send her soul to rest, Lord send her soul to rest.
4. God bless your house, your children too, Your cattle and your store; The Lord increase you day by day, And send you more and more, And send you more and more.

Sussex Mummers Carol. C.M.   THE YULETIDE SONG AND CAROL BOOK © 2014 DAN HARPER

46. This Endris Night

Traditional
English carol, 15th century

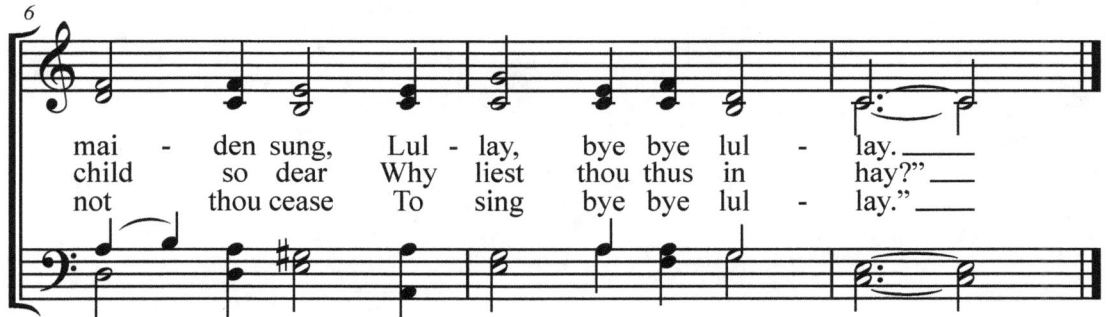

1. This en-dris night I saw a sight, A star as bright as day: And e'er a-mong, a mai-den sung, Lul-lay, bye bye lul-lay.
2. This love-ly la-dy sat and sang, And to her child did say: "My son, my son, my child so dear Why liest thou thus in hay?"
3. "O moth-er mild, I am thy child, Though I lie 'midst the hay But ne'er-the-less, do not thou cease To sing bye bye lul-lay."

Alternate words by William M. Crane:

1. Ye shepherd plains of Bethlehem,
That rest in silence long,
Break forth your Christmas echoes, till
All hear the angels' song.

2. Ye shadowed homes in lands oppressed
By centuries of wrong,
Let heavenly gladness enter in
For, hark, the angels' song.

3. All ye who hear from far and near,
The Christmas joy prolong;
Learn in the fulness of your hearts
To sing the angels' song.

4. Ye wider plains of neighbor lands,
Ye hills and mountains strong,
Take up the sound and everywhere
Repeat the angels' song.

5. Ye busy towns and cities vast,
With all your hurried throng,
Calm now your noise and tumult, while
Ye learn the angels's song.

47. Today Be Joy in Every Heart

Frederick Lucian Hosmer, 1877 English trad. melody, adapted

1. Today be joy in ev'ry heart, For lo, the angel throng, Once more above the list'ning earth Repeats the advent song.
2. "Peace on the earth, good will to all"— Before us goes the star That leads us on to holier births And life diviner far.
3. O ye of strife, forget today Your harshness and your hate; Too long ye stay the promis'd years For which the nations wait.
4. O star of human faith and hope! Thy light shall lead us on, Until it fades in morning's glow And heaven on earth is won.

DORKING. C.M.

TWELVE DAYS OF CHRISTMAS

2

49. Watchman, Tell Us of the Night

John Bowring, 1825   Lowell Mason, 1830

1. Watch-man, tell us of the night, What its signs of pro-mise are.
2. Watch-man, tell us of the night, High-er yet that star as-cends.
3. Watch-man, tell us of the night, For the morn-ing seems to dawn.

Trav-eller, o'er yon moun-tain's height See that glor-ry beam-ing now.
Teav-eller, bles-sed-ness and light, Peace and truth its course por-tends.
Trav-eller, dark-ness takes its flight, Doubt and ter-ror are with-drawn.

Watch-man, doth its beau-teous ray Aught of hope or joy fore-tell?
Watch-man, will its beams a-lone Gild the spot that gave them birth?
Watch-man, let thy wan-d'rings cease, Hie thee to thy qui-et home.

Trav-eller, yes, it brings the day, Prom-ised day of Is-ra-el.
Trav-eller, ag-es are its own, See! it bursts o'er all the earth.
Trav-eller, lo! the Prince of Peace, Babe of Beth-le-hem is come.

WATCHMAN. 7.7.7.7.D   THE YULETIDE SONG AND CAROL BOOK © 2014 DAN HARPER

3. Frankincense to offer have I,
Incense owns a Deity nigh
Prayer and praising, all men raising,
Worship God most high.

4. Myrrh is mine, its bitter perfume
Breathes a life of gathering gloom;
Sorrowing, sighing, bleeding, dying,
Sealed in a stone-cold tomb.

54. While Shepherds Watched Their Flocks

Nahum Tate, 1702

William Tans'ur, 1740

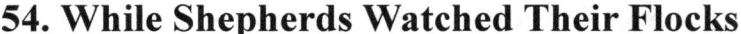

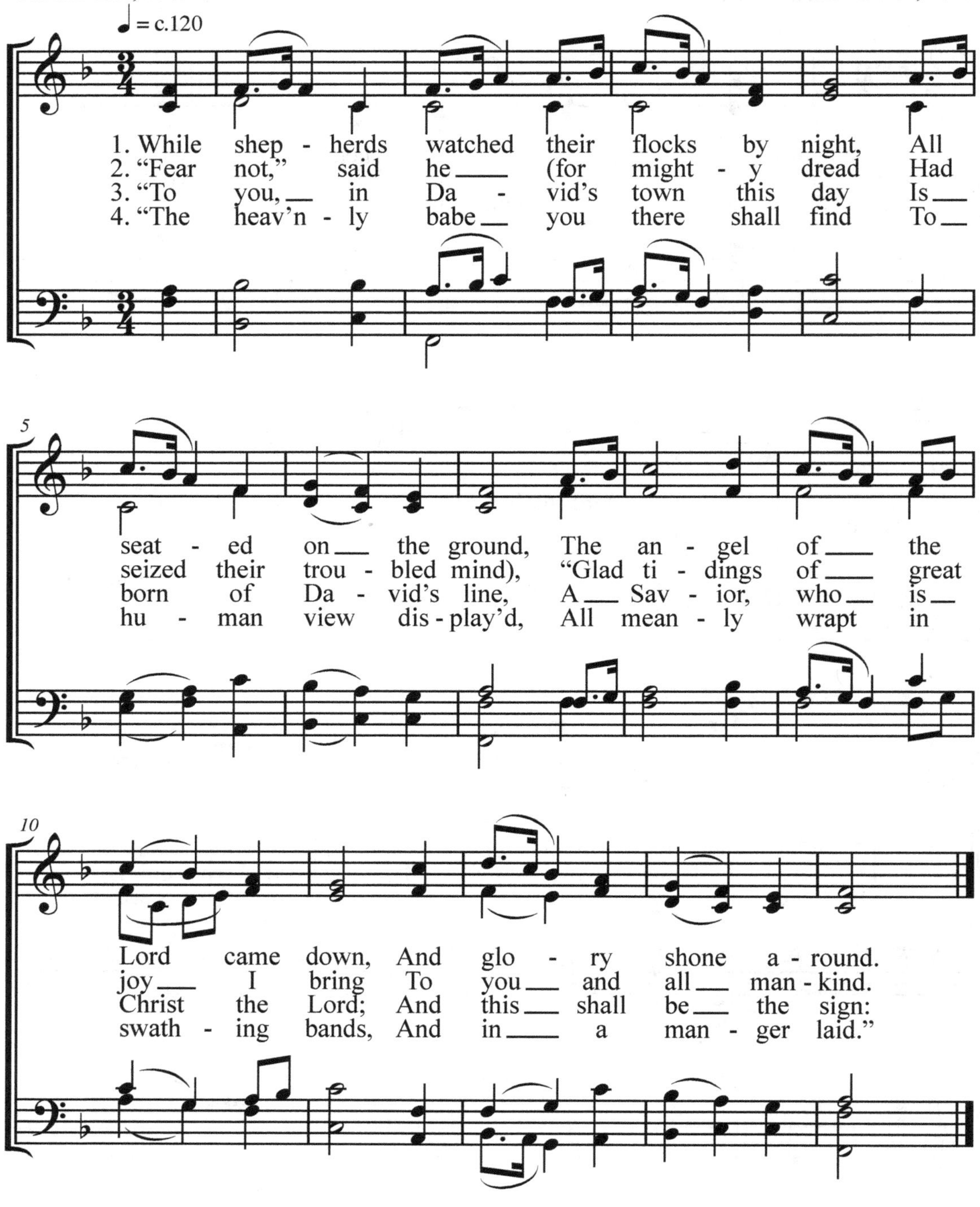
♩ = c.120
1. While shep - herds watched their flocks by night, All seat - ed on the ground, The an - gel of the Lord came down, And glo - ry shone a - round.
2. "Fear not," said he (for might - y dread Had seized their trou - bled mind), "Glad ti - dings of great joy I bring To you and all man - kind.
3. "To you, in Da - vid's town this day Is born of Da - vid's line, A Sav - ior, who is Christ the Lord; And this shall be the sign:
4. "The heav'n - ly babe you there shall find To hu - man view dis - play'd, All mean - ly wrapt in swath - ing bands, And in a man - ger laid."
5
10

5. Thus spake the seraph: and forthwith
Appeared a shining throng
Of angels praising God, who thus
Addressed their joyful song:

6. "All glory be to God on high,
And to the earth be peace;
Goodwill henceforth from heav'n to men
Begin and never cease."

ST. MARTIN'S. C.M.

55. Winter

Isaac Watts, 1719
Daniel Read, 1785

Melody is in the tenor.

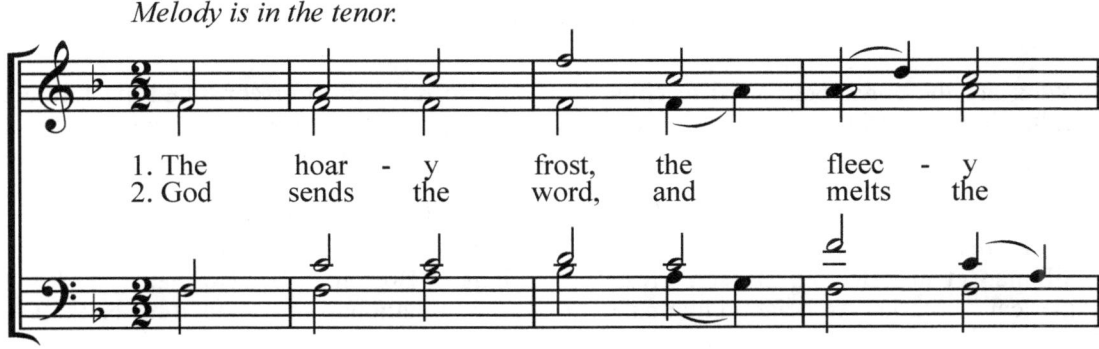

1. The hoar-y frost, the fleec-y
2. God sends the word, and melts the

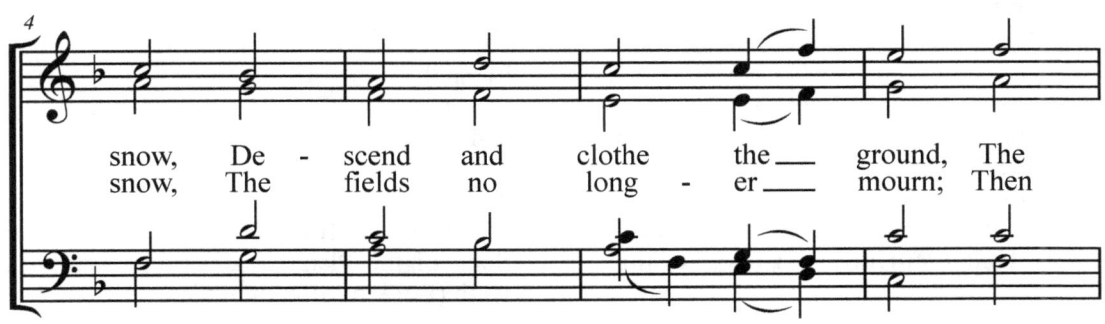

snow, De-scend and clothe the ground, The
snow, The fields no long-er mourn; Then

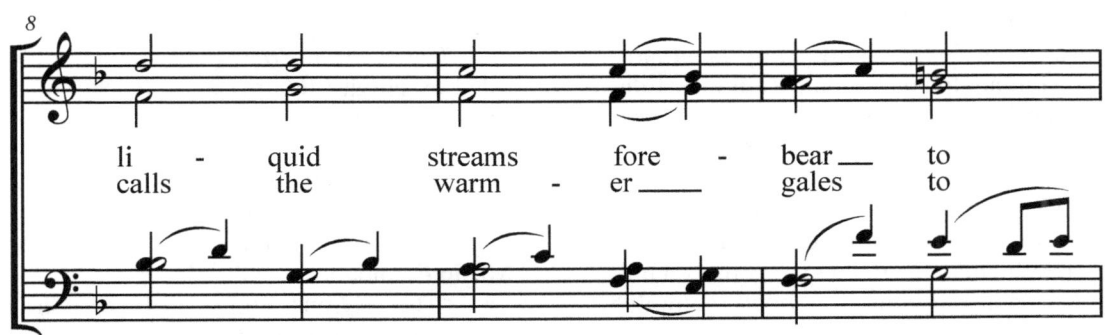

li-quid streams fore-bear to
calls the warm-er gales to

flow, In ic-y fet-ters bound.
blow, And bids the Spring re-turn.

WINTER. C.M.

Bibliography

The following are the core books used to compile this collection (listed in chronological order of publication):

The Beacon Song and Service Book for Children and Young People, compiled by Vincent B. Silliman et al. (Boston: Beacon Press, 1935); American Unitarian Association hymnal.

Hymns of the Spirit for Use in the Free Churches of America, compiled by Van Ogden Vogt, L. Griswold Williams, et al. (Boston: Beacon Press, 1937); American Unitarian Association and Universalist General Conference hymnal.

We Sing of Life, compiled by Vincent B. Silliman et al. (Boston: Beacon Press, 1955); American Ethical Union hymnal.

Hymns for the Celebration of Life, compiled by Kenneth, Patton et al. (Boston: Beacon Press, 1964); Unitarian Universalist Association hymnal.

How Can We Keep from Singing, compiled by Waldemar Hilleman, et al. (First Unitarian Church of Los Angeles, 1976); independently produced hymnal.

Songs of the Spirit, compiled by Janet Norton, et al. (Philadelphia, Penna.: Religious Education Committee of Friends General Conference, 1978); Friends General Conference song book.

Rise Up Singing: The Group Singing Songbook, compiled by Peter Blood and Annie Patterson (Bethlehem, Penna.: Sing Out!, 1988/1992); non-religious songbook compiled by two Quakers.

I also referred to or consulted the following for arrangements, texts, additional songs, and/or general background:

The Suffolk Harmony: Consisting of Psalm Tunes, Fugues, and Anthems, by William Billings (Boston: J. Norman, 1786); non-denominational song and tune book; available online through the Library of Congress Web site.

The Southern Harmony and Musical Companion, compiled by William Walker (Philadelphia, 1854); non-denominational song book and hymnal.

Christmas Carols, New and Old, compiled and arr. by Henry Ramsden Bramley and John Stainer (London: Novello, Ewer & Co., 1867); non-denominational song book.

"Go Tell It on de Mountains! A Christmas Song of the Plantation," arr. by Harry T. Burleigh (Belwin Mills Publishing, 1917).

American Folk Songs for Christmas, ed. and arr. by Ruth Crawford Seeger (New York: Doubleday, 1953); non-denominational song book.

The Sacred Harp (Denson edition), compiled by Hugh McGraw et al. (Carrollton, Georgia: Sacred Harp Publishing Company, 1991); non-denominational song book and hymnal.

"Digital Tradition Folk Song Database" (Web site), hosted on www.mudcat.org, compiled by Dick Greenhaus, et al. (Mudcat Café Music Foundation, 1988-2014).

"The Hymns and Carols of Christmas" (Web site), www.hymnsandcarolsofchristmas.com, compiled by Doug Anderson (1996-2014); includes multiple variants of certain texts and scans of old Christmas song books.

"Hymnary" (Web site), www.hymnary.org (Grand Rapids, Mich.: Calvin College / Christian Classics Ethereal Library, 2007-2014); page scans and other information from approximately five thousand hymnals.

.

HOLIDAY INDEX

General seasonal
Jingle Bells 27
O Tannenbaum 36
Winter 55

Christmas shopping season
Jingle Coins (parody) 28

Advent (four Sundays preceding Christmas):
O Come, Emmanuel 33
Watchman, Tell Us of the Night 49

Posadas (December 16-24):
Posadas, Los 38

Yule and Solstice:
Boar's Head Carol 4
Deck the Hall 11
O Tannenbaum 36

Christmas and Christmas Eve:
Angels We Have Heard on High (1st) 1
Angels We Have Heard on High (2nd) 2
Away in a Manger 3
A Child This Day Is Born 6
Boar's Head Carol 4
Children, Go Where I Send Thee 7
The First Nowell 12
The Friendly Beasts (1st) 13
The Friendly Beasts (2nd) 13
Gaudete 15
Go Tell It on the Mountains 16
God Rest Ye Merry, Gentlemen (1st) 17
God Rest Ye Merry, Gentlemen (2nd) 18
Good Christian Men, Rejoice 19
Holly and the Ivy, The 22
I Heard the Bells on Christmas Day (1st) .. 23
I Heard the Bells on Christmas Day (2nd) . 24
I Saw Three Ships 25
It Came upon the Midnight Clear 26
Joy to the World 29
Lo, How a Rose E'er Blooming 30
Mary Had a Baby 31
O Come, All Ye Faithful 32
O Little Town of Bethlehem (1st) 34
O Little Town of Bethlehem (2nd) 35
Once in Royal David's City 37

Rise Up, Shepherd, and Follow 39
Shepherds, Shake off Your Sleep 40
Sherburne 41
Shiloh 42
Silent Night 42
Star in the East 44
Sussex Mummers Carol 45
This Endris Night 46
Today Be Joy in Every Heart 47
We Wish You a Merry Christmas 51
What Child Is This? 52
Whence, O Shepherd Maiden 53

Christmas Day
(suggestions for daytime celebrations):
Boar's Head Carol 4
Children, Go Where I Send Thee 7
Gaudete 15
Go Tell It on the Mountains 16
I Heard the Bells on Christmas Day (1st) .. 23
I Heard the Bells on Christmas Day (2nd) . 24
I Saw Three Ships 25
Joy to the World 29
Today Be Joy in Every Heart 47
We Wish You a Merry Christmas 51
While Shepherds Watched Their Flocks by Night 54

St. Stephen's Day (December 26):
The Cutty Wren 10
Good King Wenceslas 20

Holy Innocents (December 28):
Coventry Carol 9
Mary Had a Baby 31

Twelfth Night (January 5 or 6):
Cornish Wassail 8
Here We Come A-Wassailing 21
Twelve Days of Christmas, The 48

New Year's Eve (December 31):
Deck the Hall 11

Epiphany (January 6):
We Three Kings 50
Mary Had a Baby 31

GENERAL INDEX

First lines of songs are in quotation marks. Where first lines and song names are the same, only song names are given.

Adestes Fideles (O Come, All Ye Faithful) . 32
"anges dans nos campagnes, Les" 2
Angels We Have Heard on High (1st) 1
Angels We Have Heard on High (2nd) 2
Away in a Manger 3
Boar's Head Carol 4
"boar's head in hand bear I, The" 4
Bring a Torch, Jeanette, Isabella 5
Child This Day Is Born, A 6
Children, Go Where I Send Thee 7
Cornish Wassail 8
Coventry Carol 9
Cutty Wren, The 10
"Dashing through the snow" 27
"Dashing through the mall" 28
Deck the Hall 11
First Nowell, The 12
Friendly Beasts, The (1st) 13
Friendly Beasts, The (2nd) 13
Gaudete 15
"glorious angel from heaven came, A" 45
Go Tell It on the Mountains 16
God Rest Ye Merry, Gentlemen (1st) 17
God Rest Ye Merry, Gentlemen (2nd) 18
Good Christian Men, Rejoice 19
Good King Wenceslas 20
"Hail, the blest morn, see the great
    Mediator" 44
Here We Come A-Wassailing 21
"hoary frost, The" 55
Holly and the Ivy, The 22
I Heard the Bells on Christmas Day (1st) 23
I Heard the Bells on Christmas Day (2nd) ... 24
I Saw Three Ships 25
"In the name of heaven, I ask you
    for shelter" 38
It Came upon the Midnight Clear 26
"Jesus, our brother, strong and good" 13, 14
Jingle Bells 27
Jingle Coins (parody) 28
Joy to the World 29
Lo, How a Rose E'er Blooming 30
"Lullay, thou little tiny child" 9
Mary Had a Baby 31
"Methinks I see a heavenly host" 42
"Now Christmas is comen" 8

O Come, All Ye Faithful 32
O Come, Emmanuel 33
O Little Town of Bethlehem (1st) 34
O Little Town of Bethlehem (2nd) 35
O Tannenbaum 36
"O Christmas tree, O Christmas tree" 36
"Oh, where are you going, said Millder" 10
"Oh, dsahing through the mall" 28
Once in Royal David's City 37
Pilgrims, The 38
Posadas, Los 38
Rise Up, Shepherd, and Follow 39
Shepherds, Shake off Your Sleep 40
Sherburne 41
Shiloh 42
Silent Night 42
Star in the East 44
Stille Nacht 43
Sussex Mummers Carol 45
"There's a star in the east on
    Christmas morn" 39
This Endris Night 46
Today Be Joy in Every Heart 47
Twelve Days of Christmas, The 48
"Un flambeau, Jeannette, Isabelle" 5
Wassail Song, The
    (Here We Come A-Wassailing) 21
Watchman, Tell Us of the Night 49
We Three Kings 50
We Wish You a Merry Christmas 51
What Child Is This? 52
Whence, O Shepherd Maiden 53
"Where are you going, said Millder" 10
"While shepherds kept their watching" 16
"While shepherds watched their
    flocks by night" 41, 54
While Shepherds Watched Their
    Flocks by Night 54
Winter 55

www.ingramcontent.com/pod-product-compliance
Lightning Source LLC
Chambersburg PA
CBHW081348040426
42450CB00015B/3344